I0029301

JOHN THE COMMON WEAL

JOHN
THE COMMON WEAL

BY

HENRY NOBLE MacCRACKEN, PH. D.

CHAPEL HILL
THE UNIVERSITY OF NORTH CAROLINA PRESS
LONDON: HUMPHREY MILFORD
OXFORD UNIVERSITY PRESS
1927

MANUFACTURED COMPLETE BY THE

KINGSPORT PRESS
KINGSPORT, TENNESSEE
United States of America

CONTENTS

JOHN THE COMMON WEAL

INTRODUCTION

FOUR hundred years ago, when William Tyndale's translation of the Bible enabled every man to interpret God's will, when Martin Luther defied spiritual authority in the name of the individual conscience, a poet of Scotland created a personality uniting in himself the welfare of a whole land. Sir David Lyndsay of the Mount was a herald at the court of James V. When in poetic vision he symbolized all Scotland in John the Common Weal, he was more truly a herald than he knew—a herald of the dawn of nationality in world history, a forerunner of the age when folk of all estates would recognize their mutual obligations for the improvement of society. For the first time in history, so far as I know, Lyndsay saw a nation incarnate in one man, and created a character beside which John Bull, Uncle Sam, John Company, and the rest are mere caricatures.

Lyndsay's John the Common Weal was a son of the Reformation. He may justly claim

to be the first messenger of the gospel of social welfare. The character appears in two
poems, one called *The Dream,* written in
1528, and the other called *A Satire of the
Three Estates,* a play produced before the
king twelve years later, in 1540. In both
works John the Common Weal speaks out
boldly of the harm done to the welfare of the
whole nation, by the lack of social coöperation. Group against group, estate against estate; that was the obstacle then, and is today.
In *The Dream,* which was Lyndsay's first
complaint against the times, John the Common Weal complains bitterly against the in-
justices of the age; and despairing of any reform, he prepares to emigrate over-sea. I
suppose it was to France or to Ireland, since
emigration to America had not then begun.
No doubt, the ancestors of many citizens of
North Carolina were, like my own, in the
company of John the Common Weal, when
they fled in hope from the abuses of Scotland to the new plantations in Ulster.

In the later poem, *A Satire of the Three
Estates,* John the Common Weal (who seems
not to have emigrated, after all, but like

Robert Burns, to have missed the boat) boldly and robustly brings his indictment again before King Humanity against the three estates of the realm, the nobility, the clergy, and the merchant class. He charges them with failure to maintain the commonwealth; his charges are sustained, and reforms are promised. It was not long after, one recalls, that John Knox, a human embodiment of John the Common Weal, began the transformation of Scotland from a quarrelsome group of warring feudalities into the energetic and constructive nation that it has since remained. At the same time another John the Common Weal, John Calvin, created almost single-handed the unified city state of Geneva, and organized its industry and welfare.

Borrowing this leaf, then, from the book of the Scottish poet, I would beg your indulgence to set up John the Common Weal again before your minds as the individual citizen, whether of today or yesterday, in whose life and opinions is bound up his country's well-being. I ask you to hear his complaint, and to discuss with him one or two ways of life which may ameliorate his hard condition.

One thing is certain in a democracy. It is the citizen, that counts. If he is afraid, we have a panic in Wall Street. If his crop is too big, he can't sell it. If he is not interested in the government, the government grows worse. If he is interested in it, the government may be improved. If he pays his taxes, his money will be good. If he fails to pay his taxes, his government goes bankrupt. We may argue as we please about the social unions to which he belongs; we may talk in technical language of the class war, the industrial revolution, the problems of city life and country life. Everything comes home, at long last, to the citizen.

It is easy to object to such an assertion. "Your citizen," one will say, "is merely a philosophical conception. No such person exists. There is no such thing as the average man. It is impossible to generalize about human beings in general, even about Americans. We are too much creatures of circumstance for any such speculations to be indulged in. Confine your observations to

North Carolinians and New Yorkers, if you please, to college men and college women, by preference, and you may say something to the point. But the time is past for ill-grounded speculation on a conventional symbol. John the Common Weal is a myth."

Perhaps it may be so. John the Common Weal may be just a myth after all, although in every comic newspaper we quickly recognize by symbols national figures much less definite than his. But after analysis has set apart and classified individual traits, is there not left a residuum of common human need and aspiration in us all that is still worth our consideration? Public opinion may be as ill-informed and prejudiced as some writers affirm it to be; but nevertheless it exists; and nothing is more surprising in America than the unanimity of its expression. So far as it exists, American democracy is based upon it. We are a country of large majorities on one question or another at one time or another. There must, therefore, be some general inclinations running through our population of which we may take account. The most dangerous of all generalizations is perhaps the fear of generalizing.

It is, at any rate, this real if vague generality of human nature in America that is to be connoted in the figure of John the Common Weal. He brings his complaint against his times; and his times will answer him that the fault lies not in his stars, but in himself, that he is an underling. We shall find that if John the Common Weal is to have the kind of a country he wants, he will have to take upon himself the training that will make him capable of getting it. In seeking an outlet for public service he will learn that there is provided a laboratory of citizenship, in which the loyalties to which he pledges himself call him to make a more valuable use of his leisure. And we shall observe that running through the whole of American life there is a certain active principle of neighborhood, which thus far has delayed the segregation of our people into classes and groups, sects and castes; which, in a word, keeps us all Americans, and makes public welfare a living principle. This principle, whether incorporated in the body politic, or definitely organized in voluntary trusteeship, or left spontaneous as time and occasion may evoke it, is susceptible of development through a plan of education that is America's gift to the world.

I. THE COMPLAINT AGAINST THE TIMES

CHAPTER I

THE COMPLAINT AGAINST THE TIMES

SOME day the United States will have a bureau at Washington, which may go by the name of Anthropometeorology, the Bureau of Human Weather. The Department of Commerce aspires even now to something approaching this function. Business statistics, however, all-embracing as they are, do not yet comprise the whole horizon of man's kenning. The tides in the affairs of men must be charted by experts in sociology, in education, and in psychology, as well as in economics.

The trade-winds of commerce and peaceful work blow with fair steadiness through the years and down the centuries. Westward they take their way; and the sails of many a good ship of state have bellied out, while the bow dipped toward the sunset where the

alluring gold of Ophir seemed to lie. But
every once in a while, from causes no less ob-
scure than those that breed the West Indian
hurricane, there spring up before the fright-
ened eyes of the nations whirlwinds of human
passion. The process of their growth is less
known than is that of the cyclone, although
some men, like Pitirim Sorokin, who have
lived in the heart of such human storms, have
tried to describe their passage. Sorokin, a
Russian social revolutionary and private secretary to Kerensky in the first popular government of Russia, has written a book called
The Sociology of Revolution, which is an
essay toward the charting of this new human
meteorology. He, himself, tried to ride out
a gale of human anger, and was, when I first
met him, an exile at Prague, but his ship
came to harbor in the University of Minne-
sota, far from the madding tempest. His account is supplemented by many others, though
few are as well-trained to observe. It is clear,
at least, that like Benjamin Franklin's note
of the real cyclone, the greatest velocity of
human opinion may go directly counter to
the general movement of the whole spirit of

the age. In the human weather chart we call such currents winds of reaction, counter-revolutions. Those who live in such times are very apt to think that the world, as they rashly call their little "syllable of recorded time," is going backwards. Then the winds die down, the storm subsides, the skies clear, the steady winds of trade fill in the vacuum caused by the wild tempest, and men and women go about their lawful occasions. Windows are glazed again, roofs are reshingled, débris dumped in the bay, and at last the town of Mansoul takes on its wonted appearance. Somewhere, it may be, at such times a poetic lad may find, like the survivors of the "twilight of the gods" of Norse legend, a set of golden chessmen in the grass; and new games, new poetry, again delight mankind. We have not drifted so far backward, after all. Some saving instinct of self-preservation has wrought for man.

Such a human hurricane tore its way through the continents of Europe and Asia for ten years, from 1914 to 1924. America has heard the fame thereof with its ears. Its exact place of origin no man knows; but the shrewdest guessers place it in the same great plains of Asia whence so many tempests of the past have come their twisting way. The pressure of empire, Russian and British, engendered hot winds of intrigue that began it. Germany suffered from Hamlet's complaint, and was "too much i' the sun," without having sufficient place in it. Precursors of the great storm were seen in the first and second Dumas of Russia, the first and second Balkan tempests over Turkey. And then, suddenly, the great wind came howling and crashing upon us.

Now it has passed. We men and women, lifting our heads cautiously, scarce realizing we are the survivors, go about the town, wondering, wondering. What has happened? What shall we do? Can we build better against the next storm? Can we do away with man-made hurricanes altogether? At least, can we not chart their course, if they have one, and give storm warnings sufficient to take adequate precautions? So that in the next cyclone of destiny, it may be, the loss of thirty millions of men and a hundred millions of children shall not be the toll left in its dread wake? There are some that have no faith that we can. No reconstruction of society, according to their view, can be built that will stand the onset of human passions. Lisbon, San Francisco, Yokohama and Miami may, by taking thought, defy the earthquake and the wind, but the cataclysms peculiar to men are beyond the power of men to resist. Acting upon this theory, they then proceed as rapidly as possible to provide dynamite with which to make the next shock more terrible. Many other human engineers believe that a structure guaranteed against shocks can be erected. Many plans have been proposed. The League of Nations, a world pool of raw materials, a system of world free trade, disarmament, a world pool of debts, a world religion of peace, a world league of youth for peace, a world league of women for peace and freedom, an international language, an international Red Cross and social service,—these are some of the methods proposed for strengthening our fragile human structure. It will be observed that all of these plans depend upon organization. Men and women must get together.

But the difficulty with all these ideals is the instability of the foundation on which the far arches rest, of international good-will. One after another the leaders of humanity are despised and rejected by the very men in whom they had trusted. Nations cannot go very far in international understanding if they do not understand themselves thoroughly. And we turn back to education as the agency which is the only force capable of reaching the deep foundations and building solidly upon them the bases of a future world order.

No chain is stronger than its weakest link; and no government is better than its worst citizen. For one needless death, one false education, one human wreck in the path of society, the Lord will require an accounting at our hands. We have got inspection in our factories in which an axle is measured and tested to the thousandth part of an inch; we have practically no inspection at all for John the Common Weal. He comes unbidden and departs unsped. We think gladiatorial shows and bull-fights cruel, but every city in America is a slaughterhouse of needless deaths.

If men had always talked of automobiles there would have been no improvement in the product. It was when they began to study a particular car, and one single part of that car, that improvement began. A man is not a machine, but if we gave him half the care we give our machines, he would be more of a man. We shall never know the essential, indestructible, common nature of man, the true John, until we have patiently analyzed and measured with scientific method the incidental influence of history and political organization; of village, county, and state; of every social condition; and have learned from this study how much environment may or may not do, and how far it may be controlled in man's interest.

We want America to be better, but do not think of America often enough in terms of John the Common Weal. If he is unhappy, if he is wrong-minded, then everything is wrong. We may rail at him, as our critics do, for his instability, we may solemnly state that his mentality is that of a twelve year old child, but that does not help us. If he really is what they say he is, why then he is, you may depend upon it. Well, we must begin from there; and try to see what can be done to bring him into good condition, whether it be by the imperious direction of a ruthless doctor, or by self-discipline.

Whether or no John the Common Weal can truly analyze his ills, he at least knows there is something wrong, and today he brings his indictment against the government no whit less severe in its arraignment. For our national Congress he has scarce words enough to express his contempt. His most scornful epithets are reserved for that body which, by all precedent, should be held most in reverence, the United States Senate. John the Common Weal despises his government today and cares little who knows it. George Bernard Shaw used to say, "Those who can, do. Those who can't, teach." It is a commonplace of our professional jesters in America that those who can't are elected to Congress. "Some day, Jimmy," says the proud mother of a current jest, "if you make enough money, you can get elected to the Senate." There is no barometric arrow so sensitive to public opinion as the joke. But who is to blame, the

government or John himself? John stays
away from the primaries and election booths,
voting at the village polls once in four times;
he elects every other president, and when he
deigns to vote he often seems to care more for
the badge he wears than for the issues presented to him. The most scandalous mal-
feasance in the offices of the government
seems to have no effect in alienating him
from his traditions. So the vicious circle is
continued, by returning unjust men to power,
whose continuance in office evokes renewed
contempt.

For the foreign policy of his government
he seems to care even less. He rails against
it more or less frequently, especially when he
looks for it and cannot find it. Once in a
while he wonders what has become of the
treaty of Lausanne. Sometimes for a moment the words Tacna-Arica in the newspaper excite a fleeting memory of something
our government was engaged in a short time
ago. "Whatever became of it?" he asks, and
then immediately forgets that he has asked
the question. Yet history will record that at
Tacna American diplomacy met its severest

test in the American hemisphere. He is surprised to learn that our trade with Russia is some fifty million dollars larger each year than it was before the war. He had known somehow that we did not have anything to do with Russia. The American Federation of Labor, he recalls, has promised to protect him from the insidious wiles of the Muscovite. But here he is with a trade of two hundred millions with a country that he had thought he didn't speak to! Curious!—and then he forgets all about it. The one hundred and fifty millions of Russian Peters and Pauls dealing over the counter with our John the Common Weal, and all the while Peter and Paul and John won't speak to each other. John's self-sufficiency encases him in thrice-bound indifference.

Occasionally John's heart is stirred by the news of an earthquake in Japan or in Armenia, by a flood or famine in China, or a plague in India. Then he settles down again to the inertia of his comfortable isolation. The oceans make most comfortable pillows for him.

That is, they would be comfortable, if life

were only quiet at home. But unfortunately John is subject to nightmares. He rubs his eyes as he reads about the frightful tale of homicide and crime in his own land. He has killed tens of thousands of his fellow-citizens in accidents in the last few months, and many other thousands in anger. His thefts and dishonesties clog the courts. The laws he doesn't like he wilfully disobeys, and he defies his government to make him respect them. And then when things go wrong and he is put in a position of discomfort, he cries to Heaven against the government and brings his indictment against the Constitution and the laws. Who is to blame for what has happened,— the governor of the state indicted for mal-administration in office, or John the Common Weal who has carelessly chosen him? Do they not, at least, share the blame?

One thing is clear, John the Common Weal of these United States cannot, like his predecessor, emigrate. There is no Ireland or France to be possessed by a conquering race. His empire in Central America and the Philippines is not colonizable. He cannot escape from the conditions he himself has created;

he can only turn upon himself and ask what has made him so unhappy, so dissatisfied with his condition; and set about to remedy it within the limits of his own township.

"The proper study of mankind is man," but man was a long time in finding it out. Or rather, man failed to remember that the man he should have studied was himself, and not his ancestors. For every study of contemporary life in our colleges and universities there are ten courses in the distant past. I have recently had occasion to review the statistics of the study of sociology in American colleges. There is in my office an immense chart showing the courses given in most of the older institutions, prepared for me by a reseacher in sociology, Mrs. Elsa Butler Grove. From a half-hearted study chiefly along economic lines they have grown into the well-developed and well-organized departments such as we find in the University of North Carolina. No other discipline offers such wide variations in its course of study; and yet in most colleges there seems no well-thought plan for the student to follow. We have at least, however, a beginning of the study of the interplay between man and the conditions that have made him, from which, after diagnosis, we may arrive at a prescription. Such a study begins, I suppose, in social geography, in comparative human physiology, and rises from the analysis of soil and climate, mountain and plain and sea, through the physique and organism they have developed, to the social psychology of the groups of men. When history is properly taught, it will be taught, no doubt, in terms primarily of sociology.

The suggestion made by Professor Meiklejohn of the University of Wisconsin, that in a college students should study in some such way the development of the world of the Greeks and then follow it with a similar study of the development of the English, has much that is suggestive and provocative of thought. Those civilizations are sufficiently remote from our own, sufficiently distant in time for us to get some perspective upon them. We can ascertain motives that began to rise from life upon a narrow peninsula in the midst of a great sea, or from life generated in an island that was the ultima thule of civilization.

Even more stimulating, I should think, from the sociological point of view, might be the study of the Northmen. They, too, were isolated by fiord and ice and fjeld, by mountain and stormy sea, by fiery volcano and drifting ice. Out of this isolation we see created physical hardihood and courage, handicapped always by the emotional excess of social repression in such lonely lives. Through a violently homicidal community there gradually worked the strong roots of a society of law; and, unlike the civilizations of Greece and Rome and of England, there gradually developed conceptions of those qualities of essential manhood which all respect. Not that in the other civilizations such qualities did not exist, but through the development of class rule the authority of law was found in the perpetuation of institutions, rather than in the character of the leader. The Northmen lived, too, in village communities, more nearly resembling our American hamlets.

Sociology has had some influence upon our study of such history and of the classics; and there is no part of the American curriculum today that is unaffected by it. We cannot study the spectrum without thinking of the elements there disclosed and of the uses to which humanity has put them. We read literature in the light of its social background. The most popular courses in the Greek and Latin Departments found in the college catalogue are under such titles as "Greek Life," and "Society in the Augustan Age." Our whole curriculum is being socialized, through the emphasis placed upon the study of contemporary man which sociology has demanded.

But however valuable the study of past civilizations, no study, I believe, can compete with the study of American society in value to the college student. There are too many factors which can find no counterpart in other civilizations. Let us take, for example, the fact of immigration which has played such a great part in the structure of American society. I am not thinking primarily of the immigration from European shores, vast as that has been, and without precedent in Great Britain or in Italy. That immigration has now, for a time at least, come

to an end; and our people have declared for
the principle of self-increase. But there still
continues throughout three million square
miles of our continental territory a vast emigration, a shifting population with a mobility
for which there is no precedent in world history. The statistics of passengers carried
upon our railroads are beyond credence, to
one who reads them for the first time. It
would seem that all America was awheel.
With an automobile for every five citizens,
the entire country rolls off on rubber. With
the creation of cities like Los Angeles in a
decade or two, the emigration of a million
people to a single center is a commonplace in
our history. Gigantic booms, such as that
in Florida, rise and collapse without greatly
affecting John the Common Weal. We have
grown so used to the phenomenon that we
think nothing about it. A foreigner stands
in amazement some evening in the Union
Terminal in St. Louis and watches the great
Pullman trains, section after section, gliding
off like snakes from a den down their num-
berless tracks. In Europe, between Vienna,
a city of two millions, and Prague, a city of

a million, scarcely two hundred miles away, two sleeping cars suffice to carry the night travelers. Between Boston and New York, a dozen trains of several sections each, ten to fourteen cars in length, pull out every night with every berth taken. Such a factor as this incessant emigration and interconnection of every part of the land is a phenomenon simply without precedent in other countries. Its causes and its effects must be studied by our own sociologists, and utilized in the analysis of the principles that make for the integrity of American life. If, in Europe, society is founded upon stability within certain districts, American life must be founded upon mobility; and the fact must be taken into account. The present speaker represents on his paternal side seven generations of Scotch-Irish ancestry in which no son ever lived in his father's house beyond the age of nineteen; or in his father's city, for that matter, or in his state. And this history is typical of vast masses of his countrymen. The continuity and stability derived from permanency cannot be depended upon to keep American life integral. New factors must be found to supply this want by social alignment and by education.

The nations most famous for survival, such as the Brahmin race of India or the Jewish race, have made much of nomenclature. They have preserved the family names unchanged through hundreds of years. Their genealogies run back through the centuries. In America it is not simply the wise child that knows his own father—it takes a historian to remember his grandfather. I should doubt whether one American in a thousand knows the family surname of his grandmother. The very fact that in our public libraries genealogies are the books most in demand, attracts attention not to the facts which Americans remember, but to those which they have forgotten. With the successive waves of emigration that have swept across the country an increasing degree of anonymity has resulted. Prefixes and suffixes are dropped, and spelling follows sound in elision and syncopation. De Molyneaux becomes Mulnix, Moses becomes Morris, and in Boston the other day a Cohen became a Cabot. That stability and integrity and strength that come from a pride of ancestry and of a good name, rather to be chosen than great riches, as the proverb says, are lost in our commonwealth, which cares nothing for a man's name or birth, and asks only for material and current success.

Again, in America, we have the problem of migration, not simply in a geographical sense, but of migration from group to group. John the Common Weal is in nothing so constant as in this, that he does not propose to remain in that position in which it has pleased God to place him. About fifteen years ago in the city of Poughkeepsie where I live, a lad of seventeen bringing a heavy piece of ice into the hall of a business college dropped it on the staircase and was thrown out of the building by students, for his carelessness. He picked himself up—he had never been a student himself and had never been in school —and shaking his fist at the privileged lads who had ejected him, he shouted, "All right, you have thrown me out; but I am coming back some day." Last month, about fifteen years after that episode, that ex-iceman purchased all of the subscribers' stock in this business college and elected himself president of the institution. The iceman's name was Giovanni Mariano,—the president of Eastman Business College is John B. Marian. This episode is characteristic of the social mobility in America. American sociologists cannot find such conditions elsewhere in the world. The phenomena can be studied only in America, and for the most part only at the present time. Yet it is of vast importance to anyone seeking to analyze the causes of success and failure in the American democracy.

For such men achievement in American society is attended with very few external rewards. The rich man may build himself an expensive palatial home, but can he find anyone to run it? He may buy himself a thirty-thousand-acre tract in which to hunt in the Adirondack forests; but the natives are not likely to let him shoot over it with impunity. He may own country homes in a half dozen states, but all of these honors he pins upon himself. There is not much satisfaction in that. He wants the approval of his fellow man. He yearns for respect and honor. How can he obtain it? In other countries there

are decorations and dignities, ranks and re-
compenses of different sorts for him who has
achieved. Academies may crown his book
and signalize his service to his people. The
cynical will scoff at this evidence of people's
consideration; but no one who has ever lived
in a foreign country will deny that these
things have a practical value in attracting
the attention of people to those careers
deemed worthy, and in affording to those who
have achieved such careers the satisfaction
of gaining the esteem of their fellow countrymen. They counterbalance that over-em-
phasis on mere money-value that besets our
people.

In one or two instances, indeed, this European custom has been made international and
world-wide, as in the case of the Alfred
Nobel Prize; and in America the Woodrow
Wilson Prize, a similar reward, has been set
up. There are also the Roosevelt medals.
But for the most part our citizens labor without any recognition except that which comes
from their own consciousness and the grati-
fication of their desires. Certainly the honorary degrees which are scattered about with

profusion by university heads in expectation of further benefits cannot be classed as permanently satisfying rewards. It is a source of no little satisfaction to the supporters of Vassar that that institution many years ago declared itself opposed to granting the honorary degree. The whole system, that is to say, of social recognition in the formal creation of rank or dignity is entirely un-American. Some other motive must be substituted for this entirely worthy one, which animates so many British and French hearts. It is for the sociologists to analyze this question, and to suggest a solution.

Another American phenomenon is the loss of alien culture in the American soil. The process, often commented upon, has not yet been observed with any degree of thoroughness by well trained scientists. A French sociologist spent last year in America, in a New England city where eighty-five per cent of the population are of French-Canadian extraction, trying for the first time to put down from very accurate personal observation the process by which a French-Canadian ceases to be a French-Canadian and becomes a

citizen of these United States. This loss of
racial and national character is attended by
pathos, and even by tragedy at times. It is not
a process to which a citizen willingly lends
himself. It occurs most rapidly among children, more sensitive and adaptable than older
folks. But it is not sufficient that the alien
civilization be lost. It must be merged in
something new. The sociological question
arises, "What is that new thing that takes
its place? What sentiments are to accompany
the process?"

A student friend of mine, a Slovak, recently investigated the dietary of her fellow
countrymen in the city of Chicago. She
found that these immigrants, born and bred
in a rural life of the most active kind, climb-
ing mountains and undergoing the most rig-
orous physical labor for subsistence, were in
Chicago confined in narrow tenements, engaged in piece-work in the clothing industry
and in similar industries. They had brought
their peasant appetites with them, and grati-
fied them by huge attacks upon American pie
and hot breads. The result, as might be ex-
pected, was the most acute Slovakian indi-

gestion, and a resultant pessimism as to the value of citizenship in our republic. The sociologist, it would appear, must call to his aid the physiologist, the linguist, the student of religion, the political scientist, and the economist, if he is truly to analyze the conditions of our American life and suggest their future direction in education.

I think the migrant in this country, the migrant from Ohio to Southern California, has often stripped himself, like the red-skin whom he has deposed, of all those garments of society which have seemed to hamper him in his race for success. He has won success, and has lost the art of wearing it well. For social customs are like garments, and though many of them are perhaps incumbrances, they do protect us from the inclemency of the elements.

The American has no state religion, no economic theory for his state, no definite restriction of personal liberty and individual rights, on the basis of which his country has formed its resolution to survive. It is true that social preachers like Dr. Crothers fear the advent of a state religion which would deny the right to teach evolution or to read more than one translation of the Bible. It is true that Herbert Hoover advocates policies which come perilously close to a system of state economics. It is true that social groups acting independently and even counter to the law sometimes abridge the rights of other groups of citizens and try to force into their state government laws justifying such action. But upon the whole the American fabric of state is still bare of any integration from social institutions within the government itself. The large number of voluntary societies that hover round the capital indicates the lack of interrelation of such social groups with the government. No other country is so free of institutional control. The sociologist must realize this fact; and analyzing its cause and its effect he must try to provide in the imagination of John the Common Weal some other stimulus which will make him loyal to public service.

These and other considerations suggest strongly the importance of social science as a need to be realized in American education. If John the Common Weal is going to understand what has happened to him in this America of 1927, social science alone can get at the real truth.

Just at present it would appear that individualistic promises will defeat socializing tendencies for decades to come. The main currents of religion, art, literature, philosophy, society, are separatist in tendency. We see education itself moving in lines tending to isolate rather than to integrate the citizen. The well established doctrine of universal public education has been supplemented and to some extent supplanted by private education and even more by parochial education. Public education is for the masses only. There seems nowhere in America any great tendency to limit or to restrict such a development. Yet it is vastly important that private and parochial education, if they are to continue, shall be publicly minded, and this is not the case at the present time. The rural districts of our country in many parts become increasingly isolated in spite of the automobile and radio. The population moves steadily toward the town. In Denmark, sociologists tell us, the drift of population is the

other way, and there is no sociologist in
America who will not wish the same were
true with us. Why can it not be so? Boost-
ing is baneful. No one who has lived in con-
gested districts of our great industrial cities
can desire to see them repeated or extended.
Yet the pressure is increasingly toward the
center. A corresponding movement carries
the classes of higher income away from such
congestion into suburbs whose boundaries
are as carefully guarded as the foreign
quarter of Shanghai which no Chinaman is
permitted to enter, or the foreign park which
no Chinaman is permitted to enjoy. There
are whole cities in the United States where
citizens of non-Christian stock are not permitted to buy land. A few days ago in Philadelphia I copied down in a trolley car this
advertisement: "Linwood, the most rigidly
restricted suburb in Philadelphia." I
thought to myself that only in America could
a real estate agent advertise his town by call-
ing attention to the rigidity of its social control. Such a thing would be revolting to a
European individualist, but in America there
is a lure in the words. "How do you keep

out the Jews," my friends ask me, "at
the college?" and smile incredulously when
I tell them that we have no exclusive
policy.

No, Mr. Bertrand Russell is wrong when
he observes, as he did recently, in his book
on education that America has a true practice but a false theory. We have a true theory
but a false practice. We remain content with
a great tradition, the tradition of colonists of
English and Scottish blood. Our strongest
and most virile stock is still maintained by its
political training in supremacy over the other
races. It has the intensest loyalties to family
descent, and enjoys the prestige that attaches
to the first comer. We continue with our religious affiliations which divide our state
groups in their social activities and in marriage with the religious fold. We rest inert
beneath party banners. The two party system
is almost unbreakable in the United States,
while within each party the conflict of ideas
renders its unity very much a farce. Our at-
tachments in social terms are stronger in
these ways than is our democratic theory.

Yet they are loosening, and the sociologist

of today believes we are in a transitional period between the old and the new. The failure of great masses of our citizens to register in order to exercise the privilege of the poll, the enormous increase in breaking not merely of the law against the manufacture and sale of intoxicants but every other law, is an evidence of this weakening in the old social groupings; and I, though not a sociologist, cannot be content to see John the Common Weal in the midst of such transition unprotected and unaided in his journey along the road. It seems to me that it is the part of education and particularly of special schools within the universities to help him. We must have students in research who can describe clearly the phenomena now taking place, for in no field is there more misconception. We must have other experts trained in public health, in social welfare, in political administration, ready to step into administrative posts in the new institutions as they are formulated for the democracy of the future. And such training, it seems to me, is an essential part of a liberal education.

You may define the word liberal as you

like, the root meaning of it is freedom. The
ignorant man is never free; and no one ever
attained freedom without leisure. There is
often little that is liberal in the attitude of the
so-called liberal arts, in refusing to be con-
cerned with what is going on at the present
time. They therein show their intolerance.
Nor is science much more liberal at times in
its restriction of the word science to the data
of natural phenomena, and in its refusal at
times to follow anything from the path of
pure research into the utilities of life. There
seems to be springing up a new Puritanism in
science, no less intolerant than the older Puritanism of conduct. Here social sciences
mediate between the classical and historical
studies, and the more exact studies of nature.
They summon both groups to the service of
John the Common Weal; and, in fact, they
liberalize the American college curriculum,
since they give other studies the only measure
of conduct and life.

And if sciences like psychology and bi-
ology seem sometimes aristocratic, art on the
other hand is often timid and self-conscious.
It thinks nothing American is really artistic,

yes, often that the Oriental has said the last word about art. There is danger, therefore, of an increasing chasm between the theory of education and the life of John the Common Weal. This chasm must be bridged before it is too wide.

John the Common Weal suspects these products of the intellect, since their standards are foreign, and he is somehow placed at a disadvantage by them. Not until art has become an ingredient in our native air, will our citizen cease from his distrust. There is no country in the world where the intelligent classes are more sharply marked from the great governing groups. And it is the fault, chiefly, of the intelligent classes themselves. In art the externals of European culture are imitated; in science there is an arrogance and dogmatism quite out of keeping with the small progress that has been made. Our critics have apparently never read the fable of the traveller, the sun, and the wind. Meantime politics and public service are not held up as desirable courses for youth. Cynicism and timidity reign instead.

This, then, is the substance of John the

Common Weal's complaint against the times. The time is out of joint, and he is not yet convinced that he has been born to set it right. Persuasion of this truth must come from education; education, above all, in the social sciences.

Here and there are signs that we are about it. The call to public service has made itself heard in progressive institutions among the colleges. Elsewhere students, stirred by the message that has come to others, have issued their own summons. Interest in current issues may be suppressed by the administration; it crops out in secret meetings and in student newspapers. Students endeavor to apply theories current in public life to their own needs, and as a result have been frequently in conflict with their teachers. The movement against compulsory military training may be cited as an instance. Students are asking what there is in an intellectual life which requires the discipline of war, when the life of manual labor has no such handicap. Their protests are met with the familiar cry, "Reds! Reds!" Yet in truth Bolshevist Russia is the only other state that has mobilized its intellectuals. Are we, too, in America, trying by force of arms to put across a propaganda? If the propaganda were of democracy, one might understand it, for education in democracy is needed. But it is not, and the student movement of today is much closer to true democracy than the subversive forces trying to dominate our education.

John the Common Weal sees all this, and knows not what to think about it. He would like to escape another World War. He dislikes things as they are. But his remedy is not, as he thinks, some new law or regulation. It is something that must come from within. The experience of others, even the glorious democracy of Greece, the deliberate progress of England, will not greatly aid him. He must know himself. And in thus taking thought, he must seek counsel of the social scientist to explain his problem and to direct him out of his wilderness of worries. So much we may already see. Yet he needs immediately a laboratory of experience. Public office furnishes one way, but to a few chosen citizens only. Two other laboratories exist, in which every citizen can put to practice what he learns. They have been developed without much aid from education, and for this reason John the Common Weal can experiment all the more freely, and can, at least in his own little neck of the woods, secure some of the satisfactions that should result from the practice of democracy. To these laboratories the two following chapters are devoted.

II. LEISURE AND LOYALTIES

CHAPTER II

LEISURE AND LOYALTIES

WE have seen in becoming acquainted with John the Common Weal that no small part of the responsibility for the ills of the times must be laid at his own door. Government in a democracy rests not alone upon the consent of the governed; that does not tell the whole story. It might be more accurate to say that government in a democracy derives its energy and strength from the active participation of every private citizen in the functions of public service. Without this distribution of authority the direction of power must inevitably become a drift toward the center. A form of state socialism or of tyranny must result. As between a democracy that does not work and a tyranny that does work, I should prefer the tyranny. Fortunately, no such tyranny is forced upon us. Yet those who acclaim the toast, "Right or wrong, my country," would compel us to choose it. With such I have no patience, for they cloak with patriotism the determination to persist in wrong. When Lincoln gave back Mason and Slidell to angry, hectoring England, he said, in effect, "My country is wrong, and I must set it right." The duty of John the Common Weal lies with Lincoln, not with Decatur. John the Common Weal of the twentieth century, like his precursor in the sixteenth century, must bring his complaint before humanity as judge; but the mandate of reconstruction will be returned to him, superscribed "Physician, heal thyself."

He may find an active healing principle in that opportunity for public service which lies within the power of practically every citizen in our republic, and which in so far as men have taken advantage of it has been a preventive of undue centralization. It is that characteristic of our land which from the times of de Tocqueville has been observed as a dominant trait of the American; the habit of association of persons in private capacities for public ends. Men everywhere associate in that way, of course; it is the extent of the practice, its continuity, and its personal appeal, that marks American life. During our association with citizens of other lands in and after the World War, this capacity was most frequently commented on. The mayor of a European town said to me, "Leave an American worker here, if only to push the button. We cannot of ourselves be galvanized into coöperation." For the origin of the custom we must look back of the history of the United States to colonial days and to English precedent. Public service is deeply ingrained in English character, particularly in Englishmen and Englishwomen of the upper classes. It is for the most part, as Lowell points out, a class service. It is probably derived from chivalry, which adopted as its motto "Noblesse Oblige." But its spread in America to a degree far beyond the conditions of English life has been due to the spirit of freedom in our democracy.

The truth of this is revealed in the word leisure, which derives from the Latin *licet* meaning *it is permitted*. Leisure, in its true sense, is but an allegory of the free man in a

democracy. And in spite of the jeremiads
of many writers on American life, who la-
ment the hurry and distraction of our age, the
chief characteristic of the twentieth century
is the prevalence of leisure. The cause of
this is so familiar to you as to need only the
barest mention. It has been recently com-
puted that through the development of me-
chanical power, every citizen in this country,
man, woman and child, has now the power of
one hundred and fifty men at work for him
without his raising a finger. If ancient
Greece, as a speaker recently pointed out,
resting upon a slave civilization with two
slaves to every citizen, permitted the leisure
of Socrates and Alcibiades, we Americans
have a leisure seventy-five times as great by
the use of our Aladdin genii of industry. It
is our vanity, our timidity, our self-indul-
gence, that allows our days to be crowded with
over-activity, and makes us socially such dis-
organized communities. Leisure is ours, but
we must make reservation for it. And in the
field of industry demands for such reservation have been successful. The recent movement for the five day week is supported by

some of our most progressive employers of labor. The unorganized groups such as the women in charge of households and in agricultural labor have experienced this reduction of hours of work and an increase of leisure almost equal to that of the skilled classes in the factories. Economists of many countries are studying the results with amazement.

Even in the intellectual groups which often consider themselves heavily over-tasked, an actual study of schedules shows ample reserves of time. We have all heard the complaint of our overworked college graduate, driven from class to class by the schedule, and harassed by assignments of outside work overlapping each other. This complaint was, at least at Vassar College, completely disposed of by what is believed to be the most extensive survey yet made of this problem. Six hundred students, inspired no doubt in part by a sense of injustice, kept a most faithful record of their hours of work and play for an entire semester. The faculty agreed to take the results seriously, and the records of their diaries were tabulated by the department of statistics and published in the Vassar *Journal of*

Undergraduate Studies last June. They show not only that the Vassar students work on studies thirty-seven and one-half hours a week, or less than eight hours a day of a five day week, but that a senior who has learned the game does what is presumed to be more work in less time. There is left a large period of free action for exercise and play, for creative activity, and for those forms of public service so amply developed in American college life. Surveys for shorter periods made at other colleges are equally convincing. In no case has there been a schedule averaging as high as nine hours a day for a five day week. Since it may be presumed that those who have kept these diaries include those students who work hardest, the average results throughout our colleges may be considerably less.

The problem of leisure, then, which is to say the problem of freedom, is nothing but the problem of John the Common Weal over again. What shall a private citizen of our time make of himself? An answer, perhaps, is found in the second word of the title; in the loyalties which have sprung up in his

private life,—in the loyalties which have
manifested themselves in his life as a private
citizen. We are, all of us, capitalists; and
students of universities are the greatest capitalists of all, since the inherited wealth of
youth is theirs. There is no capital so valuable as time. College students, you number three-quarters of a million. What are
you going to do with this surplus of capital,
this store of leisure, provided for some of you
in inherited wealth, for others of you in the
free time provided by American civilization,
for others in life as it stretches on through
distant years? May I center all I have to
write upon the subject in the one word, *trusteeship?*

Leisure is ours. It is permitted *(licet)* to
us to do what we will with this free time at
our disposal, amounting, perhaps, to a
quarter of our waking hours. But free time
is already expressed for us in terms of loyalties. Most loyalties have become deep rooted
in habits greater than we can change.
Groups for whom similar loyalties have
seemed important take possession of our own
lives through the call to serve their own kind

of loyalty. Even if we accept the imperious demands of these groups for a share in the direction of our leisure, there yet remains a freedom in the obligation of trusteeship which is well worth our examination.

We are aware that the theory of a leisure class has been assailed by the sociologists, particularly by those who lean far toward socialism. But while they have been arguing the question industrial civilization has been advancing by leaps and bounds, and the high wages and the demand for labor in our times have made capitalists of increasingly larger groups of workers. Not long ago at an Eastern college Professor Scott Nearing said to the students: "One of these days the workers on the New York Central Railroad will say to the directors, 'This railroad is ours; you have played with it long enough. Our labor has made it, and we now take it as our own.'" To this statement his opponent in the debate, an attorney for the New York Central, replied: "Many thousand employees of the New York Central own stock in the railroad which their savings have purchased, and which represents the accumulation of their labor. They are not quite yet prepared to say to the directors of the railroad, 'We annihilate the value of this accumulated labor of years, and present it to the State.'"

I am neither an economist nor a sociologist; and I realize that an extended argument on this subject could easily lead me into pitfalls which the expert can only too easily dig for the unwary. But I have had some practice in seeing American communities at work; and I find the notion of trusteeship rather widely and almost universally respected.

Perhaps as I use the word the figure conjured up is of some malefactor of great wealth, whose vanity has been flattered by yond his field of experience. This figure, election as a trustee to an institution quite be- the bogy of many liberal thinkers of today, is true for about five per cent of the trustees, so far as my own experience goes. The remainder, and they are the vast majority, are quite different persons.

I have in mind one such, who stands for me as a type specimen, to use the biological term. Her mother was one of the maids at a college. She grew up as a little girl in

the halls of the institution. She became her-
self a maid. In the course of her work an
attachment sprang up between her and one of
the women professors in the institution, and
she later became the personal maid of this
professor. On the death of the professor she
was bequeathed a small sum of money; and
borrowing money to build a little house for
members of the faculty, she set up as a land-
lady, making her own beds, cooking her own
meals and cleaning her own house. One
could scarcely imagine a person with less
leisure. Yet in my experience I have never
met anyone more efficient in her chosen business, nor one with larger reserves of time to
devote to public service. She is an unofficial
trustee of her parish, a Roman Catholic
church. It is she who organized the congre-
gation and erected the church and the priest's
house, who made of the small struggling
group a large and devoted and prosperous
one. She has had sufficient leisure in politics
to attend the primaries and public meetings of her township, with the result that she
has served on the State Democratic Committee and was delegate at the late Demo-

cratic convention from her district. She was appointed by the Governor to the unpaid Board of Visitors who, in effect, are the trustees of a great asylum for the insane recently built in her county. On the public health committee and on the committee of education her name is almost always found, and recently when a state bank was started in her township she was one of two women elected to the directorate. She is undoubtedly the best known and best loved citizen of her community. Such trustees of the common weal are a necessity everywhere in our American life. They constitute, I believe, the true answer to the problem of leisure. They make possible the rounding out of our too narrow habit of concentration on our central business, into the real fulness of life. They live, in the Biblical phrase, more abundantly.

Again we find a lesson in the World War. The unification of purpose accomplished in the United States revealed to the country its own immense potentialities of trusteeship. The dollar a year man was not merely at Washington. He, and the woman too, was in every city and hamlet in the country. He made possible the production, the financing, the assembling of great forces. What a country might we become, if one-hundredth part of that energy were daily exerted toward the better integration of all factors in American democracy!

Trusteeship is nothing but an avocation made fruitful. I cannot define it, but I would describe it as a state of mind—an acceptance of responsibility for the public good made real in some social institution which by common consent lies outside the area of the institutions of government. It anticipates government, in a sense. Trusteeship puts off the evil day of bureaucracy. It provides the middle ground between the bureau expert and the people, correcting the contemptuous attitude of the one by definite control, and dispelling the prejudice of the other by a trust in character and in personality. The best example of it is, I suppose, the woman home-maker. At present she is still a volunteer worker, for judges refuse to estimate in dollars the value of her services. She is, in effect, trustee of the little family, unpaid, but entrusted with peculiar authority and claims.

It is, perhaps, because of this attitude toward her family relationship, that woman has, since suffrage, entered by preference into public trusteeship, rather than other forms of public office.

Trusteeship interpenetrates special fields of public service with different kinds of knowledge. One college trustee of my acquaintance was president of the National Chamber of Commerce, and U. S. Food Administrator during the war. He brings to the meetings of the trustees an invaluable knowledge of public affairs. Another trustee, his intimate friend, is at the present time secretary of the United States Department of Commerce. He has brought to the trusteeship of Leland Stanford University a sense of the importance of the record of our age. The result is, that his university possesses today the largest accumulation of documents on the history of the war that is in existence. This interweaving of the special field with the knowledge of other fields is precisely that force that integrates American life to a greater degree than life in other countries. While occasionally the expert re-

sents this overlapping, and wishes to be left
free to pursue his own specialty, it is doubtful if his desire is for the best public interest. He needs an interpreter. Trusteeship is
such leadership made concrete. It rests upon
public confidence in the stability, honesty, and
fidelity of the leader in public service, and
upon the value of his criticism from the point
of view of the general good, as applied to
the particular field. Experts do not like criticism, but they need it, and from one to whom
they must listen.

The first attribute of trusteeship, stability,
implies at once the strength and weakness of
this social system. Trustees who always have
their trusts in mind are apt to be conservative.
They desire the preservation of the *status quo*.
Their position has been won by their reputation for steadfastness, and they do not propose to risk it by rash ventures. In many instances their function is the execution of a
trust which is really an inheritance from the
dead hand of a donor made legal in a contract
by bequest or benefaction. In time this may
prove a real danger, as it has done in countries
of the Old World. They are now very sus-

picious of such trusts. But conservatism in the countries of the Old World is one thing and conservatism in these United States of the twentieth century is another. We can stand a good deal more of the conservatism of the ideal trustee in the vast areas of public service that still await exploitation by those who wish to make the best use of their leisure. So, though I am usually classed as a liberal and sometimes even win abuse as a Red, I want here to plead for the conservatism of the trustee so far as concerns the faithful execution of his trust. The spirit of the times, interpreted by wise judicial decisions, will alter with sufficient flexibility the terms of many deeds of trust. They are in the hands of the people after all; and it is apparent that as yet they meet the popular approval. The interpretation placed upon trusts by American judges has been fully as generous as the interpretation placed upon the Constitution by the Supreme Court, and it is apparent that under this system of interpretation a trust bequeathed by a dead hand may remain a living thing. An excellent example is that of the Thomas Thompson Trust which administers the income of over a million dollars bequeathed for the assistance of indigent seamstresses in the villages of Brattleboro, Vermont, and Rhinebeck, New York. Seamstresses are no longer indigent since they began to spell shoppe with two p's and an e. Most of this money, I am informed, is now applied for public health in both places, and the courts have sustained the use. In one of our American colleges an endowment exists for the president's office, conditioned upon the president's being always a Presbyterian clergyman. A president was recently chosen who was not a clergyman; and a lenient judge, on hearing the evidence, ruled that the board of trustees had done the best they could, and had got as near to the specified article as the times could provide. The endowment was preserved, and a layman now enjoys its benefits.

There has of late, however, been a movement to avoid even this danger, in the formation of the community trust. This plan of benefaction, fully developed in more than fifty American cities, provides a corporation of trustees in which the judiciary, city gov-

ernment, and the largest social institutions of
the community are represented. The object
of such a selection is to combine democratic
approval, integrity, and skill. Funds are bequeathed or given to the trust, for the most
part without condition, and the trustees may
make such use of the income or principal as
may be specified, but with discretionary
powers. In order to avoid the dangers of
swollen principal, the manipulation of which
might become tyrannical, it is provided that
these trusts must be disposed of within a specified number of years. It is argued in behalf
of this form of trusteeship that the trust will
not become antiquated, as it has done in the
past. In the city of the speaker's residence
is an old men's home, the Pringle Memorial,
limited to ten old gentlemen, who because of
their age and place of residence cannot by any
conceivable manner dispose of the income of
the steadily accumulating trust fund. The
famous instance of Girard College in Philadelphia, and the one hundred million Girard
Trust, and the still more famous Sailor's
Snug Harbor in New York City, with many
millions in city real estate devoted to aged sea-

men, are cases which would have been avoided
by the existence of a community trust. This
form of trusteeship originated in Cleveland,
and is due to the public service of the late
Frederick Goffe. No other movement in the
field of philanthropy has ever commanded
so immediate a response. It is the greatest
endorsement of trusteeship ever known.

If, then, it is possible to secure a wise conservatism by trust provision, the way is open
to name two other qualities equally desirable.
They are honesty and fidelity. It is a matter
of great regret that honesty is not an outstanding virtue of the American as it is of the
Chinese, the Poles, and the English. Our
country is famous for having coined the
phrase "the square deal," but it is still more
famous for such phrases as "graft," "the lid,"
and the "rake off." There is no true trusteeship where the business of a man's vocation
is mixed up with the leisure of his avocation.
The college trustee whose banking firm sells
its bonds to the college is not a trustee at all.
The trustee's reputation for disinterest can
never be less than one hundred per cent. Future training for public service must make

this absolutely clear, and render forever impossible the past abuses of the office. The legal penalties should be severe. Trusteeship and honor should be synonymous. Just as it is said proverbially in the United States that "a village is as good as its banker," so I say with greater justice that "a village is as good as its trustees." And I believe that most trustees are honorable, though often we do not give honor where honor is due.

The third virtue of the trustee is fidelity. Although the function of trusteeship is defined as an avocation, that is, as an occupation taking up the lesser part of one's active time, it must not drop to the zero point or it ceases to be trusteeship. Between the absolute zero of the absentee trustee who is responsible for most of the objections now hurled at the system, and the overbusy trustee who, having nothing else to do, makes his trusteeship his sole occupation in life, there are many degrees of trusteeship. The amount of time to be spent as a trustee will vary with the nature of the institution; but in general it is possible to define the function of the trustee so as to limit these amounts of leisure. The true function of the trustee is, we have seen, to review in a judicial capacity the administration of the trust and in the light of this criticism to authorize the future policy. The trustee, that is to say, should not be the administrator nor should he interfere with the administration. His function is, primarily, judicial; it is also, in part, legislative. If he confines himself within these limits, there will seldom be any conflict between the trustee board and its officers, or between the board and the community. Frequently, however, there is a tendency to overstep these bounds.

In reviewing the trust his first responsibility is, as I have said, to the financial terms. The trustee is responsible, in the last analysis, for the condition of the trust and of its accounts; and I think there has never been an administrative officer who in digging into the history of trustees and trusts has not found appalling instances of negligence. It is not always easy, let me say, to place the blame for this. Fidelity to terms of a trust is not so easy as it sounds. Let me give you an instance from the records of Vassar College. A gentleman, a resident of San Francisco, bequeathed to the college a scholarship fund the terms of which were, by a resolution of the Board of Trustees forty years ago, "accepted," as the minute reads, "in accordance with the terms of the will." These terms, however, were not spread upon the minutes of the board. They remained in a separate document which was lost. In the meantime occurred the San Francisco earthquake and fire, and all records of the will were destroyed. For forty years, therefore, the Board of Trustees administered this scholarship as if there were no other terms than that of scholarship aid, and when at last the heirs of the testator laid claim to the interest of the fund to aid a descendant of his, the trustees were in a quandary. They were able to secure the sworn statement of an attorney who had drawn the will, a few days before the testator's death, and accepting this as their guide they have made good the earlier dereliction. Such instances are all too common in the history of trusts. The only remedy is complete publicity, such as is given in the photostat copy at Harvard University of all trust agreements.

There is needed for trustees not only more careful preservation of records, but a complete reform in the system of accounting. Accounting has now become almost as exact a technique as science; and there is no excuse in allowing in any American community the inadequate methods which too often prevail in the care of trust funds, whether permanent or current. As the directors of a bank are responsible for the honest conduct of the bank, so the trustee should be held morally liable to the community for the guarantee of income in any year. This is one of his principal duties. He may delegate this to some professional officer; he may be relieved of it as in the case of school trustees who use funds obtained from public taxation, but he has no right to authorize in the budget any expense for which income is not provided by a plan for which he assumes moral responsibility. The abuse of this principle is seen most frequently in institutions deriving support from private benefaction. Yet they, above all others, should be administered on the budget plan. Social workers should all have a course in accounts.

And nowhere is the safety inherent in publicity more obvious than in the publication of the budgets of social institutions. If, as Professor Ripley has shown, our great commercial institutions are undermining public credit by the suppression of the true state of their finances, it must also be acknowledged that public confidence in the trusts of public service is all too often undermined by the secrecy with which they are administered. A friend of mine is intimately associated with the educational system of one of our largest religious denominations. His duties call him to all parts of the country to inspect and report upon the administration of trusts. His appointment was made necessary by the irresponsibility of trustees who under the protection of secrecy were covering up the records of improper conduct.

Publicity should be inherent in the trust agreement, primarily because the mandate of trusteeship should be popular. Whether the trustees should be appointed by the founder of the trust and thereafter coöpt its membership by vote of surviving trustees, or whether they should be appointed, as are the Regents of the New York State University, by the government, or whether they should be elected in some manner by the community, as in the case of alumnæ trustees, is not the most important point. The essential point is that they should possess the mandate of popular approval upon their appointment and that the public record of their work should be periodically presented to the public for their criticism. We do not need to have a popular election in a village to know whether the trustees of the village church are doing their duty well or ill. The community knows, and the trustees know what people think; and the wise trustee acts upon the knowledge. Personally I believe strongly in making the election of trustees as popular a process as it is possible to secure, considering the inertia of the villager in such matters. The force of a body is not equal to its mass but to mass times acceleration; and if there is no acceleration in a community from popular responsibility, there is apt to be little force in the trust.

Trusteeship has been at times opposed as

tyranny. A recent volume written by my friend Professor John E. Kirkpatrick, *The American College and its Rulers,* favors in effect the abolition of trusteeship and the transfer of the function to the workers. The evils of absenteeism, of class prejudice and self-protection, he has stated, are too great to be overcome by a sense of responsibility to the public. I do not believe this; and I cannot agree with Professor Kirkpatrick; and for two reasons. First, because I believe it to be possible by my theories of loyalties for a trustee to be chosen whose service is not bound up with his major interest in life; and I believe this to be true of most trustees at work today in the American community. And, secondly, I do not favor the transfer of the trust to its beneficiaries, because I know of no successful instance in which trusts have been so bequeathed to those for whose benefit they exist with lasting security and stability and fidelity. People will not give money to such trusts. The very idea of the trust is opposed to it. The very theory of the trust is that it is a power placed with a disinterested party for the benefit of the third party.

When John Colet founded Saint Paul's School in London he made the Mercers' Guild the trustees of the property. Their interest in the trust was certainly not that they might manufacture the clothes of the poor scholars of the school. It was, rather, that their guild was known throughout London for probity and honesty and for its care of those elected to membership in the guild.

That the trustee system is full of faults no one will think of denying. When John the Common Weal gets elected trustee he will be no better trustee than he is a man. He may be ignorant, ungallant, dilatory, arbitrary, or irresponsible, as the case may be, but such dangers and faults are not in the system but in humanity. The corrective lies in the education of the community to the qualities that should be demanded of the trustee; and in the training of educated men and women for such service.

And the public recognizes these qualities today; but unfortunately, as is so often the case, when the public has been satisfied that one man possesses all these virtues, it elects this man to all available trusteeships and then rests. There are personalities in American life who seem designed for trusteeship almost from birth. Such men are frequently broken down by overwork not in business but in the care of their community. One friend after another secures their services until finally the physician steps in and removes the offending memberships as he would remove an appendix. I know of one such experience four years ago, when overwork compelled a man to resign from more than thirty such offices in a single day. The list was appalling; and he himself had not been conscious of it until the physician probed his life. In the three years that have elapsed since he began to take care of his personal health, the memberships have come creeping back into the office file of correspondence.

There must be a wider education upon this function and more training for it in our universities, in order that the hitherto overworked trustee may be a really useful and loyal member of a few social institutions. Only a limited part of our community has the qualities needed in trusteeship, but there are enough to fill every post as yet desired. The presence of this trained group enlisted in public service would immeasurably increase the response to public improvements when needed. Every student who has enjoyed the benefit of an academic education is morally bound, it seems to me, to accept trusteeship. I would not except even an Edgar Allan Poe, or a Sidney Lanier, or a Henry Thoreau, or a Whistler, or a John Sargent, or a Joseph Jefferson, or an Edwin Booth, from the duties of trusteeship. I believe that the art of the artist would be the better if he associated with his fellow men in some such disinterested public service. I am sure that Chaucer's art was the better and more universal because of, and not in spite of, the fact that he worked in a custom-house and travelled on embassies. I am sure that Shakespeare was more tolerant and broad-minded because, as we know, he was not averse to accepting the duties of a trustee in arranging the marriage of the daughter of an old friend, and in defending the town of Stratford against the encroachments of predatory wealth. There may be temperaments unfitted by emotional instability for the responsibilities of trustee-

ship, but there is no cure for such temperaments so good as a little experience in trusteeship. I know one famous psychiatrist whose
entire therapeutic seems to consist in getting
the self-centered and emotional egoist to for-
get himself in becoming trustee of the pleasure and happiness of others. And since in
American life the demands of business are so
insistent, it is often through the existence of
trusteeships of definitely organized institutions that the American business man can get
that freedom from his office and his vocation
that he needs in order to live. How fre-
quent it is in the history of American industry
that just as the rich man is planning to "pull
down his barns and build greater," that very
night his soul is required of him!

Of trusteeship as a stepping stone to public
office only a word need be said. The transition is slight. The competency needed is the
same. The public confidence is equally essential. The public office is then indeed a
public trust; and one who is accustomed to
think of such labor in terms of disinterest can
more easily continue in that mind than one

who depends on political salary for his living.

The most notable recent instance of the American trustee is Jeremiah Smith of Boston, trustee of Hungarian finance for the League of Nations. His labors were completed in a spirit of the highest ethics, and he refused even his proper compensation. Another recent instance is the labor of Charles P. Howland for the League of Nations, in supervising the transportation of Greek refugees from Turkey.

The code by which such men have worked, and have brought honor to their country, is a code known and understood among us; and deserving of much wider application, particularly among the youth.

Some of the other dangers of trusteeship are beyond the limits of this study. The election of a man to trusteeship merely because he is rich is a fault of American society, again not inherent in trusteeship but simply an evidence of gross materialism which puts a premium on his riches rather than on his character. But there may come about an education in trusteeship which will remedy this fault. The elder John D. Rockefeller once told me that he accepted trusteeship at Vassar College without much thought of public service, but that while he visited the college one day he met William Harper, then Professor of Hebrew at Yale. This chance meeting of the master in industry with a wonderful personality in education led to the founding of the University of Chicago on its present scale, and what is more, to the creation of the great educational and research foundations which were the outgrowth of his benefactions. I should not advise a board of trustees to elect a rich man just because he is rich; character should be the prime desideratum; and the public has a right to demand it.

I have referred to the very real danger of electing as a trustee a man with no vocation, or a man who has retired from business. This seems to me a doubtful practice, for such a trustee is apt not to stop with his functions of review and authority, but will often attempt to usurp administrative functions, and to limit the officers responsible to the corporation for the exercise of their duties. He is also apt to be arbitrary, and override the established codes of practice. The other members of the board may correct this evil; but usually it is accompanied with friction. It is most often found with the aged trustee; and for this reason I would urge that every trusteeship should be upon a term basis, and that a man should retire from trusteeship when he retires from active business. It may be possible to maintain his usefulness in a consultative capacity thereafter.

But whatever disadvantages exist in the system, such disadvantages are far outweighed, it seems to me, by the importance of such service, not only to the individuals who assume it but as an example to youth and as a corrective of the materialism which must inevitably run through industrial civilization. The reactions of honest trusteeship are profound. I know of one active trustee, for example, whose business it is to advise great corporations upon their attitude toward the public and upon their financial methods in securing funds. The value of his advice consists only in the fact that he considers himself in the capacity of trustee for the public. His advice is never in the sole interest of the company who retains him but in the interest of the public. He is standing today squarely in the path of a group of men trying to secure a great amalgamation of railroad systems by methods which he considers improper. He has no financial interest in the transaction. There is every reason why he should stand aside and let things take their own course. Every reason, that is, but one. His sense of responsibility as a trustee, knowing what he knows, is so great that it directs his action. His trusteeship in a business capacity has grown, not out of his vocation, but out of his public service as a trustee, and of his high conception of the duties of one who acts in the interest of others.

I would not close this account without a word of recognition of one whose long life of public service has just ended: Louisa Lee Schuyler. During the Civil War she was one of the women of the North who organized the Sanitary Commission, an association which anticipated the Red Cross, in which she later was a leader. In New York, her home, she founded and was one of the trustees of the State Charities Aid Association which has overcome the inertia of the public in its responsibility for the care of the insane. She founded the Association for the Prevention of Blindness; and laws have been passed through her efforts in this great work. To the end of her long life she accepted one trusteeship after another and was ever faithful to her trust. Her works were imitated in every country. She was by common consent the leading woman of New York State. Miss Schuyler was the great-great-granddaughter of General Philip Schuyler of Revolutionary fame and the great-granddaughter of Alexander Hamilton. She was not less a public servant than were her great ancestors in the public offices of war and peace, in the defense of the commonwealth in arms and the defense of its Constitution before its legislative assemblies; her trust was less spectacular, but equally needed for the common welfare.

Scattered over our land in every village and every hamlet there are today others like her; the trustees of the public library, of the public and private school, of the college and university, of the church and the benevolent society. In the cities are serving the trustees

of the great community trusts, one or two
of them possessing funds amounting to one
hundred million dollars; and in the great centers of population are the trustees of the great
national foundations.   There are also the directors of the community chest, a plan widely
adopted, which coördinates solicitation and
concentrates responsibility.   We have long
ignored the value of voluntary service in
maintaining the welfare of our democracy;
we have failed to recognize what it has con-
tributed in unpaid and unrecognized benefit
to the common weal.   We have, therefore,
failed in our system of education to include
this function as one of the prime duties of a
citizen.   Let us trust that this deficiency in
American education, this blindness in public
opinion, may soon be remedied.

In the hands of untrained men and women
the trust may be a menace, not a blessing.   As
an incentive to the right use of leisure it is too
valuable an aid for education to disregard.

III. NEIGHBORHOOD

CHAPTER III

NEIGHBORHOOD

A GOOD word is a nut full of meat. Its full flavor and utility are not to be guessed at from mere outward form. Like the stones and the running brooks, there are many sermons in a word.

Neighbor is such an one; and so is its derivative, neighborhood, which is here employed in its abstract sense, the condition of being a neighbor, and not so concretely, as is usual in North Carolina, the area inhabited by neighbors. "It is two neighborhoods from here," said a North Carolinian recently in answer to an inquiry of distance. The older meaning is less definite. To be a neighbor is just to be a "nigh" or "near" "boor." That is the etymological history of the word. So you see that a neighbor is a very common person who lives near you. Certainly, a boor is a man reduced to his lowest terms. The root of the word refers to tilling the soil; and is accordingly a near relative to the universal copula *to be*. The German for peasant, *Bauer,* and the Greek word from which *physics* and *physiology* are derived, are the same as this term of common and universal existence.

John the Common Weal brought over from England a pleasing use of the word "common." Common, too, needs explaining. In parts of the country districts a man is still described as a common kind of man, when the speaker means, affable, approachable, unpretensious. Two other words have been associated with it which have also friendly meanings. These are "clever," which in the country sense means good-natured, and "homely," which in the country meaning signified membership in the family. Such rich terms, supplementing the terms friend and home, indicate how great a premium the Anglo-Saxons have placed upon these qualities. Rich compliments may be implicit in being called common, clever, and homely.

Neighborhood, then, may be taken to mean the recognition of the community or common

interest which is involved in the mere nearness of existence. It is the ultimate basis of
society, and the only real one. All others are
artificial. To make it, as I would do, the essential ground of all public service, is to rid
oneself of a good deal of specious rationaliz-
ing, and even of hypocrisy.

Social psychology, which is the basis of
sociology, is only the application of the laws
of mind to the conditions that spring from
neighborhood. It is, indeed, not so much an
application of psychology, as psychology itself; for man's mind was not meant to be
alone. It works only in association. Man
alone is abnormal. In so far as our world
has restricted neighborhood, in so far it is abnormal and wrong. The road to sanity is the
road back to neighborhood. This is not ro-
manticism, but plain scientific fact. War,
competitive economic strife, class friction,
sectional prejudices, denominational bigotry,
race hatred, and most of the other collective
ills of mankind are only the results of
bringing dissociated groups into collision.
The good neighbor will go with none of
these.

But sociology is more than social psychology. It is social history, too. It is moral custom and folk-life. Psychology is a key that unlocks the door to the social conditions, but the field extends indefinitely. When, as in the recent work of J. A. Hadfield, *Psychology and Morals,* psychology passes into an analysis of religion, it goes far afield; and it is a question whether at this point the strict scientific method of pure psychology is longer available. Mental hygiene, or psychiatry, is equally on the border-line of science. Alexander Macleod's book, *The Mental Hygiene of Jesus,* shows how closely the great religious leader's thought is paralleled by exact scientific diagnosis.

This middle-ground between science and religion is the chosen field of sociology. Less exacting in the terms of its experiments, less devoted, perhaps, to the minute specialization of experiment, more cognizant of factors of time, of space, and of variation, sociology appropriates freely the teaching of religion without fear or prejudice.

The Christian religion is preëminently the religion of neighborhood. Confucius taught

it; the Buddha enjoined it; Mohammed com-
mended it; Jesus alone defined it, practiced
it, and analyzed its very essence. When the
self-justifying member of the legal profession tried to trick Jesus into a position unten-
able in the light of Hebrew law by asking
him "Who is my neighbor?", the Master cut
the Gordian knot of the intricacies of all the
conflicting schools of his day by a single
stroke. He outlined the character of a Samaritan. The world added to the character,
by universal consent, the epithet "Good," a
word Jesus had reserved for Deity. To be
"good" is still to be a Samaritan.

As a result Samaritanism is the name employed in Europe, and particularly in France,
for a certain ethical principle. The Good
Samaritan is the perfect example of the true
neighbor. And because of the connection of
sociology with religion, instead of attempting
a scientific analysis of a field, I should like to
pause for a moment to describe a man in the
terms of the familiar story.

The Good Samaritan was a perfect neighbor, because he was actually near to the man
who was bound for Jericho. No other

thought occurred to him than the thought *"There* is a man in trouble and *here* am I."
He never interposed the thousand reasons which would have justified him in abstaining from relief, such as must have been advanced by the Priest or the Levite. For though a physical neighbor for the moment, he was not a real neighbor in the philosophical sense, for the Jews had no dealings with the Samaritans. It was the easiest thing in the world for a man of that speculative age to reason that though near in the body, yet he was truly not near in reality, for the realness of a Samaritan was not that of a Jew. That is the way many of us reason today about Japanese, for instance. But no metaphysical speculations, no political, social, or religious convictions got into the way of his straight thinking that he was a neighbor of the suffering fellow-traveller upon the Jericho road.

The man of Samaria recognized the immediacy of neighborhood. In that lay his opportunity. Time as well as space was in the reality of the occasion. Neither he nor the man might ever come this way again, nor

˙ might pass one another upon the road of life. For a few seconds only, as he jogged upon his horse down the steep winding road through the Judean hills, was he to be the neighbor of this man. If neighborhood was to be a real experience for him, it must also be immedi-ate, and he must act immediately, or the opportunity would be forever gone. Most men would have been promptly inhibited by the very rarity of the occasion. "This, too," they would have said, "will pass." The man from Samaria, on the other hand, was stimulated. I remember years ago, when the myth of the Yellow Peril first entered sociology by way of Kaiser Wilhelm the Second of unblessed memory, an American defined China as "not the Yellow Peril, but the Golden Oppor-tunity." The definition still holds good, in spite of the desperate straits to which our attitude toward Russia and the Eastern nations has driven our international diplomacy. The Golden Opportunity is still with us, and we are wasting it. It is a pity that impractical Samaritanism should not be the policy of our very practical State. It prefers the Yellow Peril to the Golden Opportunity, because

then you know what you have got. Hatred
is tangible, war is real. Peace is imaginary,
good-will intangible. Not so reasoned the
Samaritan. To him neighborhood was the
only reality.

He recognized also the inevitableness of
such neighborhood in life. It is impossible
that this occasion of need had been, or was to
be, the one instance of neighborhood in the
career of the Samaritan. It is, rather, described by the Evangelist (a physician, by the
way) as his ordinary way of action. He was
a habitual traveller; he would come this way
again, as he told the landlord of the inn; and
since such episodes would occur again at any
time, he might then be the sufferer and his
Jewish neighbor his rescuer. Neighborhood
is inevitable, and though the moments of it
are golden opportunities and no single moment is repeated, yet no day is without them.
It is hard for us to encase ourselves against it.
What is more, it is useless.

The man of Samaria went a step further.
He was disinterested; he asked no questions;
he secured no bond from the one benefited.
He did not even seek to know the name of the

injured man, but incurred duties and debts
beyond his own immediate capacities, delayed
his own business, and laid himself open to
the charge of violating immemorial custom
in the interest of mere common humanity.
Such risks are at times far more dangerous
in consequences than maltreatment at a rob-
ber's hand. For anyone to advocate the recognition of the principle of the international
neighborhood of Russia is to incur a charge
of Bolshevism. The Samaritan was very
likely debarred by caste, because he had
touched a Jew. Yet I dare affirm that the
primary international function of government is not the promotion of trade, but of
human intercourse; that "recognition" as a
weapon of trade is a dangerous perversion of
democratic practice; and that this country
will one day have bitter cause to regret the
surrender of the peace-making function of
Congress to the State Department and the
President, in making and unmaking government in Central America, in menacing South
America, and in dickering for trade with the
bribe of recognition all over the world. Far
better just to recognize the fact of neighbor-

hood, and to find other means of protection if that be essential.

The neighborhood that asks "What is there in it for me?", the modern advertising that has accomplished the prostitution of the beautiful Old Word "service," these are false and meretricious. The man from Samaria did not tell the landlord to inform the man from Jericho who it was that had taken care of him; he did not ask that a memorial tablet be erected by the roadside to commemorate the event, he did not base his accounting practice with the fellow-traveller on the Jericho highway upon his capacity to pay, ultimate or approximate. He merely said, "When you have done what you can for this man, keep the bill; you know me, and I will pay it the next time I see you." The event as told by the Master was businesslike, in the best sense; and this very businesslikeness of the whole transaction is a spirited contradiction to the sentimentalism of some of our public servants.

Note also that although the Samaritan acted from the most definite of platforms, the mere physical fact of his own physical nearness to another man, and that man in need;

yet the action which resulted from this minimum of human understanding was broad, nay, universal in its scope. I had rather have a man live freely from the most limited theory of life, than that he should live narrowly and selfishly from the most liberal of platforms. Too often we are taught to live in an atmosphere of cant. High-sounding generalities are our stock in trade. Tolerance and liberality, generosity and benevolence, are the commonest terms of our American life, and we are often urged to live in accordance with these great truths. The men who hold my respect are those who look out greatly from more simple and more restricted points of view and who, in living in accordance with the thing they greatly believe, are themselves the living illustration of a great ideal.

A certain kind of tolerance is just insufferable patronage of superior persons, as if the Pharisee had shown his virtue in recognizing the publican. Such people tolerate others because the contacts are infinitesimal, and because the moment of contact, fraught with no social consequences at all, will soon pass.

They tolerate because they don't care. No issue is at stake. True tolerance is the motive of a busy life, not the indifference of idle leisure. A Vassar professor said not long ago in an address: "We all know what we mean by the open mind. We mean the mind that has nothing in it." Toleration too often partakes of such open-mindedness.

It is a point also worth making, though one should not push a parable too far, that the Samaritan acted with skill. His remedies for wounds were the best in his time, and not very different from the best in our own. The wine to sterilize, the oil to reduce chafing, these are still standard practice. Neighborhood is never the worse for knowledge,—a cardinal principle of sociology.

Finally,—for we must not dwell all the evening with our friend, the Samaritan,— we should observe that he accepted the full responsibility of what was implied in his physical nearness to his unnamed neighbor. These responsibilities resulted from the simple application of the Golden Rule which is the fundamental axiom of sociology. Nothing was complicated about the whole matter. The social nature of man being recognized, and mutual aid accepted as a necessary principle of life, his physical neighborhood suggested that his manhood should carry on where the other man's strength had failed; and the action was as swift as his thought. The Biblical narrative rightly puts the whole story in a single sentence: "And when he saw him, he had compassion on him, and went to him and bound up his wounds, . . . and put him on his own beast, . . . and brought him to an inn, and took care of him." It was all one act. One step followed the other without question or pause.

Too often in the American neighborhood inhibitions of fear and doubt get in their work between the first impulse of pity and the common actions of humanity that should succeed to it. We lose initiative, and so forego the minimal vestiges of decent human behavior. Such action should be ingrained in our national life so deep in the wood that no possible abrasion will ever cut them out. It was this loss of momentum, and not any purposed betrayal, that caused the failure this autumn of the appeal of the American Red Cross for Miami.

It has been my experience that the really generous people of the world, the ones really self-sacrificing and devoted to public service, act in precisely the manner which we find to be true of this citizen of Samaria. When they are confronted with an opportunity, their response is instant, whole-hearted, and without thought of the morrow. Refusing to weigh the remote possibilities involved in their actions, they are faithful to the utmost upon the most limited basis of neighborhood. I would not choose to set out on an Arctic adventure with any other kind of men, and why should I choose that most dangerous of all explorations, life, with anyone else? There is no other honest platform for dwellers in our world.

There was once a philosopher named Plato, who set out upon an adventure in government with a friend whom he thought to be worthy of his trust. It was to be a grand experiment, the first time in the world that a state had been ruled by philosophy. Romantic optimism ran high. The result was disaster, from two causes; the unworthiness of Plato's partner, and the philosopher's compromise with his own principles.

In our own day, once again, the grand experiment is being tried. Czechoslovakia, a nation of thirteen millions, has chosen a philosopher as its head. Dr. Thomas G. Masaryk will, in my humble opinion, take rank one day with the great statesmen of the world. No leader ever had greater problems or fewer resources. No leader ever made less compromise with his principles. He has surrounded himself with scientists. He is giving applied sociology, as understood today, its first great national application. He believes the ills that bring in communistic wars of class are social in origin, and are to be prevented, not by oppression, but by social education in a scientific manner. In the midst of his busy life, he finds time to philosophize, and his views are the wisest and sanest in Europe. In a condition of hectic national feeling, he has insisted upon neighborhood as the essence of diplomacy. He put his country in debt to alleviate social ills. Calumny has touched him, but he lives serene above it, a living ex-

ponent of Plato's faith, that the philosopher-
scientist, with courage and steadfastness, and,
perhaps, some luck, can create a nation.
Such statesmen as Masaryk represent the
theory of Samaritan citizenship in world re-
lations. Their lives are consistent. They
apply to foreign policy the same personal
honor and loyalty that they practise in their
own lives, in their own communities. Yet
how few there are who follow such models.
The course of our own country has been by
no means so consistent.

John the Common Weal often makes the
old error of the beam and the mote. The
United States lectures Europe about the unsatisfactory basis of the treaty of Versailles,
and says very little about the unsatisfactory
terms in its own peace with Turkey, not yet
ratified after four years of delay. We use
harsh words about the French administration
of their dependencies, but we paint our behavior in the Philippines in the rainbow
colors of the commercial traveller. England's imperial policy is questioned by our
lovers of freedom; and we have learned from
our own official investigator what excellent

rubber can be grown in Mindanao if only
the Mindanaonians can be persuaded to grow
it with their labor and to our profit. We
carry on well organized support of foreign
missions and then fail to apply the spirit of
missions at home. We say that we keep clear
of foreign entanglements, and get our feet
bogged in the mud of Tacna-Arica. In short,
our national neighborhood is full of glowing
terms like the friend of humanity in the famous poem of the Anti-Jacobin in the eigh-
teenth century, and our actions are just about
as generous as his. The poem parodies not
only the romantic philosophy of the age of
the French Revolution but the classical ro-
manticism that affected the metres of Hora-
tian odes. It is so perfect an answer to senti-
mentality, and so little known, that I cannot
apologize for quoting it, as a converse por-
trait to Samaritanism.

THE FRIEND OF HUMANITY AND THE
KNIFE–GRINDER

Friend of Humanity

"Needy Knife-grinder! whither are you going?
Rough is the road, your wheel is out of order.
Bleak blows the blast; your hat has got a hole in't,
So have your breeches!

"Tell me, Knife-grinder, how you came to grind knives?
Did some rich man tyrannically use you?
Was it the squire? or parson of the parish?
                    Or the attorney?

"(Have you not read the 'Rights of Man,' by Tom
    Paine?)
Drops of compassion tremble on my eyelids.
Ready to fall, as soon as you have told your
                    Pitiful story."

Knife-grinder
"Story! God bless you! I have none to tell, sir,
Only last night a-drinking at the Chequers,
This poor old hat and breeches, as you see, were
                    Torn in a scuffle.

"Constables came up for to take me into
Custody; they took me before the justice;
Justice Oldmixon put me in the parish-
                    Stocks for a vagrant.

"I should be glad to drink your Honour's health in
A pot of beer, if you will give me sixpence;
But for my part, I never love to meddle
                    With politics, sir."

Friend of Humanity
"*I* give thee sixpence! I will see thee damned first—
Wretch! whom no sense of wrongs can rouse to ven-
    geance—
Sordid, unfeeling, reprobate, degraded,
                    Spiritless outcast!"
        (*Exit in a transport of universal philanthropy*)

The essence of neighborhood is not such
sentimentalism as that. It is, as I have said,
the recognition of the minimal basis of com-

mon interest. What that minimum is may well be a matter of dispute, but certain parts of our common heritage no one will deny. The arboreal characteristics of what Clarence Day calls this simian world can be easily deciphered in the comic sheets of the Sunday newspapers. They are the simple emotions of fear and pleasure; curiosity and the sense of novelty seen in groups that gather to watch an excavation; the thrill of danger and dramatic fear that appear in our love of horseplay and the antics of human flies and parachute jumpers; our love of superiority accounting for our pleasure in the misfortunes of others. These are universals and proper to the *genus homo,* which Lilly in his Latin grammar defines as a noun common to all men. This common basis of life is bounded on all sides by the degree to which social custom has extended. The boundaries are marked by education, religion, and government, by heritage and tradition. The Priest and Levite of the parable were unable to break these bonds. The Samaritan used them as a free man. It is the episodes of nature that make the whole world kin,—birth and death

and marriage, windfall and bankruptcy.
These occasions cancel all barriers, and at
such times the Colonel's lady and Judy
O'Grady are truly sisters under their skins.
In the crises such as sickness and catastrophe,
poverty and isolation, the reality of neighborhood is revealed, and no matter how thick
our veneer of sophistication, no matter how
ancient our tradition of group solidarity, our
essential humanity breaks through and dic-
tates our actions at such times.

The profession of social work has endeav-
ored to keep before the minds of the intelligent groups the consciousness of the recurring
character of such occasions. Isolation in
country districts is a current phenomenon. It
is found even in the congestion of the city
where in the middle class tenements people
live for years on the same landing without
even speaking to one another. Out of the
recognition of these occasions in which the
common need is known have arisen the social
movements of the community. The efforts
for community arts, the little theaters, the
public concerts and the library, and the social
committees; these retard the crystallization of

American life in social groups according to economic and religious standards. They render more flexible the fringes of those groups in contact with one another, and thus reduce friction between group and group.

And in the country districts the revival of folk-arts and dances, the development of such assemblies as old home week, the putting of new life into the decaying county fair, are all products of our American habit of getting together. We are not far from the pioneer after all. May the day be far distant when our enjoyment of common human interest is reduced to the vanishing point where every American does not respond.

Such institutes as this of Sociology in the University of North Carolina, under whose auspices these words are printed, have as their goal not the mere recording of the social life of the people of this state, their methods of organization and action, their custom and tradition. Their mission is rather by the assembling of their knowledge to enrich the life of the community, to point out its needs, to provide the means by which those needs can be satisfied. By such efforts provincialism need no longer be dreaded. The community will not fall back into ways of indifference. The inroads of industrialism can be tempered if not checked. The love of beauty and need for society of every individual can be in some measure satisfied through social action. By such satisfactions the drift from country to city can be retarded, if not, indeed, turned in the opposite direction.

There are signs that forces are at work in our social life that need such studies. American society more and more tends to assign to the police the function of the individual citizen, in the occasions suggested by neighborhood. In refusing to recognize its responsibilities we are in danger of producing a Balkanized life. We talk about Balkanized Europe with its little nations and its little villages hostile to one another, districts in which people living on one bank of the stream talk one language and those on the opposite side talk another. Such a district is Teschen, which I traversed in August of last year. But what about our own Balkanized life? If the principle of neighborhood is forgotten, we shall have the same conditions.

I would not be misunderstood at this point. I am not opposed to governmental participation in social work. The very reverse is my position. I strongly advocate departments of social welfare in state and national governments. I favor training all government officials in the principles of social service. I commend especially the training in applied sociology of all policemen and policewomen. But beyond all formal social work that government can ever do, there remains the fact of neighborhood; the duty of the individual to play his part in the social welfare of the nation, which the individual citizen can no more shirk than he can shirk his duty at the polls; or in support of law and order at all times. Government participation in social work, in a community that was not itself fully socialized, would be futile. Such a community would be the victim of bureaucracy. And I rejoice that our American community has as yet not gone far in this direction.

Let me take, for example, the county in New York State with which I am acquainted. In its southwestern corner there are extensive brickyards affording employment to a

nomadic population of negroes and poorly
paid white laborers, who live on a scale not
sanctioned by morality or religion, and whose
obedience to the law is enforced only when
their actions endanger the citizens of other
groups. A few miles to the east, in the foothills of the Berkshires, dwells a population of
mountain whites, where mortality is high and
suffering is great. In the very shadow cast
by the morning sun from those hills, great
estates are far flung over the county both along
the majestic river which is its boundary and
the streams that come down to it from the
foothills. These estates are not the acquisi-
tions of the newly rich but are the inherited
properties of generations. Yet there is practically no contact between valley and hill.
Another section of population is maintained
by service in connection with the great railroad and river, and great highways through
which streams of automobiles pass. The mass
of the rural population is supported by
dairies and orchards whose products are
shipped to New York City. Still another
factor is afforded by the state institutions for
the insane and the criminal, the camps and

homes, the schools and colleges, and other social institutions that dot the landscape. Factories are found, not only in the larger centers, but in the smaller villages as well. Near the large towns suburbs are cropping out over the neighboring hills where the small gardens of the truck farmers recede. All these different groups in the community are divided by sectional and political feeling and by religious and fraternal organizations. They rarely come together.

But yet the county is, it seems to me, a pretty good place in which to live, because it has the beginnings of a common consciousness astir within its people. The recent decision of a Judge of the Supreme Court who refused permission to a divorced father to remove his son from the county to New York City so that he might lead a better life, is supported by the vote of most of the citizens. Poughkeepsie, the judge said in his decree, was a good place to live in. So it must be so. What makes it desirable? Well, just the neighborhood which arises out of physical nearness. The fact that we all live in the same area presents certain problems which are tackled by us in general groups. It is physical nearness mixed with the absence of something better to do which leads the aristocrats of the great estates to sit on cracker barrels in the village grocery stores and talk politics to the leaders of village sentiment. It is not, I regret to say, their academic training that has done it. A result of this is that a grandson of the Vanderbilt family now represents the county in the State Legislature, a scion of the famous family of Hamilton Fish represents us in Congress, a grandson of Darius Ogden Mills is at this very moment (October, 1926) campaigning for the governorship on the Republican ticket. Franklin Delano Roosevelt, two years ago, was honored by the Democratic party by nomination for Vice-President of the United States. All these young men entered politics from neighborhood as a basis, and the county is proud of them.

When the Roman Catholic hospital of the county seat was in need of additional funds a few years ago, they were provided through the efforts of a committee partly of Protestant citizens. When the county health association had to get its program before the farmers, it was the Grange that opened its doors. The Community Theatre of the county owes its existence to the direction afforded by the colleges and schools, and a bankrupt village factory has been revived and set going by a group of men from the city, chiefly out of this feeling of neighborhood. The defunct county fair was reëstablished on a new basis, more intelligent than that of the past. Even the ancient prestige of the county in the breeding of cattle has been revived by its most recently acquired citizens; and in one or two cases the prize herds of the country are now within its borders. The county is outstanding among the counties of the state, simply for the reason that the principle of neighborhood has been more fully recognized by its citizens than in most other places.

I know there is a strong feeling, among the very best minds of the nation, that all this social coöperation needs no stimulation, and no direction. "I do not believe in social work," Secretary Hoover once said to me. "Pay workmen high enough wages, and their social condition will take care of itself."

That is the gospel of American individualism, eloquently preached by the Secretary. What he really objects to, I believe, is the making of social work a mere profession, without creating it also as an art in the lives of common people. He has no objection, I know, to the public health officer, the nurse, the welfare superintendent. He does object to the commitment of the ideal of happiness to government officials, because this is the denial of the American principle of initiative. For vague and indefinite social work, amateur and spasmodic, inspired by inchoate emotions of pity and romance, I have as little use as anyone. But the ideal community is to me that one in which skilled professional officers carry out the social obligations of protection and prevention, sustained by an awakened public conscience and voluntary effort on a basis of neighborhood.

I have referred to the origin of social work in this recognition of neighborhood. It is very difficult to obtain a good definition of this profession. A friend of mine, obtaining her doctor's degree in Paris, was asked for a definition of it which the professors at the

Sorbonne might use. The one which she incorporated in her doctor's dissertation was: "Social work is that function of society that relates the dissociated individual to those institutions of which he is in need." Modern social work goes, perhaps, further than this in making of every individual that comes within its observation a special case, and in revealing to that individual, as a result of its study, methods which make possible his own reassociation. But however we define it as a science, it is the recognition of the actual dissociation of the case from average reality which is the best justification of its work. If it goes beyond this need, there is the immediate danger of professionalism which robs social work of its vitality. I have been often offended of late in my own connection with social workers by a new word which has been added to their cant terms. This is the verb "to contact." A social worker, speaking of obtaining funds, said: "I went to Mr. —— and contacted him for fifteen dollars." Just how contacting is any more scientific than old-fashioned touching is a little difficult for me to see.

There is a danger, too, of extending actual benevolence to humanity beyond the times and extent of the need. There is the danger of permanent parasitism, and a great resultant danger of patronage. There is a loss of values inherent in substituting the professional will for that of the individual. These dangers are recognized and in course of correction in the social institutions of our time.

The question "What's in a name?" was not asked by the poet in a sociological sense, but the sociologist would answer, "Everything." Anonymity is often the first stage in the individual's progress toward irresponsibility, ending in dependence and delinquency. One's name integrates one with society; and no one can estimate the amount of suffering which foreigners endure who bring strange names to our lips. The mere knowledge of the names of one's neighbors is the first step in neighborhood.

But we have other bases of the common life. There is defense, for example, and the protection of the community against danger. There is the local trade within the community. There are the special occasions. Children make a universal bond and playgrounds cut across all social barriers. So do the old people of the home and hospital, books in the village library, church and village improvement society. All of these community possessions are bound up in the good-will of neighborhood. They will endure so long as the organizations which foster them work from natural and human motives. When they are promoted by artificial means, when they are carried on mechanically by organized groups, they will lose their real value. They should never be relegated to any single group for promotion. This is at heart the difficulty with the programs of our fraternal societies. Extensive in membership as they are, they are still limited to special social groups.

The Red Cross points the way to that neighborhood which stimulates the imagination of the people of the community, and from its example I believe that international neighborhood is a possible goal. What the Good Samaritan did in Judea, the American Red Cross has done in Japan and is doing today in China. It does it because it tackles the situation on the minimum basis of human need. It seeks to go no further. It denies all affiliation of class, race, sex, or social order. It seeks only to know and to help. Other international movements, and they are legion, are attempting to follow out the same idea within other limits.

Scarcely any movement of our time is more significant than the travelling abroad of American citizens. John the Common Weal is learning new ways of travelling. We are travelling to study people, and not museums. We obtain friends rather than purchase guide books. We identify the cities abroad by the families that we know, and not as places where we saw certain statues or stained glass windows.

Keeping our identity of humanity on this minimum basis in local association, will give us the power of identifying ourselves more easily, on the same basis, in a world program and from this basis alone the international movements of the future will proceed.

We are too timid about this matter of friendship. The word has been so consecrated by tradition, in literature and history, that we are unwilling to use it for anything less than the completest surrender to a common experience. There are innumerable degrees in friendship. It is the art of life to discover them, to see how far one's mind is willing to go along with another's. For what else is insight given to us?

And now as we take leave of John the Common Weal, we see that in him is bound up the happiness of the whole people. We discover that the way of science is to analyze the particular instance, and that social welfare must adopt the method of science. We learn that the citizen cannot depend very much on the past as guide, for changing circumstances destroy the value of precedent. Our experiments must be direct and immediate, in order to be lasting. And for these experiments we need a social laboratory, such as our citizen has already found for himself in the service of trusteeship and in the simple fact of neighborhood. We are all members one of another.